The
Complete Book of
Business
Success

The
Complete Book of
Business
Success

BYRD BAGGETT

RUTLEDGE HILL PRESS®

Nashville, Tennessee

A Thomas Nelson Company

Published in Nashville, Tennessee, by Rutledge Hill Press®, a Thomas Nelson Company, P.O. Box 141000, Nashville, Tennessee 371214.

Library of Congress Cataloging-in-Publication Data Available

Baggett, Byrd.
    The complete book of business success / Byrd Baggett.
      p. cm.
    ISBN 1-55853-810-0 (hardcover)
    1. Success in business. 2. Industrial management. I. Title.
HF5386.B2274 2000
650.1—dc21

                                00-027621
                                    CIP

Printed in the United States of America
1 2 3 4 5 6 7 RRD 05 04 03 02 01 00

With heartfelt thanks to:

My mother,

BILLIE JEAN BAGGETT,

whose spirit continues to strengthen me.
May your soul continue to shine in heaven!

My father,

BYRD BAGGETT, JR.,

for his love and unwavering support.
You are a very special man, and I am blessed
to have such a wonderful dad.

ASHLEY, AMY, AND AUSTIN

—my beautiful children, who are truly
God's most precious gifts.
You each give me a powerful reason to live.

My good friend and business partner,

KEN JENKINS.

You are one of the most talented
and creative people I know. Most importantly,
your servant heart has touched my life.

JEANNE,

my wife, best friend, and soulmate.
Your faith continues to be the richest blessing in my life!

Contents

Introduction

I NEVER PLANNED to write a book. I'm a salesman.

For eighteen years I pounded the streets and managed sales staffs. And so it came as quite a surprise to realize that a simple exercise I had done for my own benefit was growing into a book. I had begun a list of habits that produce success. When I showed my list to friends, several wanted copies of their own. And when I showed it to a successful sales and marketing consultant, he advised me to look for a publisher. "The sales profession needs to get back to the basics," he stated. I agreed with him. I had begun the list following yet another boring training seminar that was long on theory but short on reality.

But business success is not only sales. It starts with leadership. That's why "Taking Charge" is the first part of this book. When I left sales to start my own business, I realized how my understanding of leadership had grown over the years while I had worked for others. All those years of watching and interacting with successful people had instilled within me a sense of what it takes to lead others and to develop a successful customer-oriented leadership style.

The leadership style that makes the most sense to me is servant leadership as developed by Robert K. Greenleaf. Larry Spears, executive director of the Greenleaf Center, identified ten characteristics of the servant-leader: listening, empathy, healing, awareness, persuasion, conceptualization, foresight, stewardship, commitment to the growth of people, and community building. This book is not an explanation of servant leadership, but a picture of it in practice.

In business, nothing happens until the sale is made. That's why the second section, "The Book of Excellence," is so important. It contains what I have learned from observing the top performers in many fields, including bankers, accountants, lawyers, doctors, stock brokers, and others. I believe passionately that these women and men have achieved their success by keeping it simple and by developing positive habits.

The key to success for individuals and businesses is satisfied customers. Satisfied customers are repeat customers. And so the third section of this book, "Satisfaction Guaranteed," contains 236 ideas to make your customers feel like a million dollars. Satisfied customers don't just happen. They are the result of truly believing that happy customers are the crucial ingredient of success and that their interests must come first. The ideas contained in this section are those used constantly by the top service organizations in America.

Taking Charge, The Book of Excellence, Satisfaction Guaranteed. Leadership, sales excellence, and customer service. These are the keys to business success. The three sections of *The Complete Book of Business Success* began as individual books. When I wrote them, I never dreamed that they would receive such international success. I have been a salesman, an entrepreneur, and am now an inspirational speaker and trainer, working with such companies as Southwest Airlines, Sprint, BellSouth, State Farm Insurance, and Synovus Financial. The ideas you will read in this book are the result of thousands of interviews and observations of the best people in the fields of leadership, sales, and customer service. These ideas, when applied, have proven to positively impact productivity, profitability, and employee morale.

There are no page numbers in this book. Start and end wherever you want. Read as much as you need to at any one time, but read these ideas often and slowly. Consider this to be your compass, always available to help you get back on track when you find yourself veering off in the wrong direction. These proven ideas will enhance your efforts whether you are a CEO or a young employee looking for success. Good luck in your pursuit of the American Dream!

—Byrd Baggett

Taking
CHARGE

*F*irst and foremost,
a good leader serves others.

*Y*our ability to
serve others starts with
mastering yourself.

*A*nswer the door when
opportunity knocks.

*M*ake finding a solution
a higher priority than
placing blame.

*S*olve today's problems
while looking to tomorrow's
opportunities.

*L*eaders visualize results.

*S*urround yourself with
talent better than your own
and carefully nurture it.

*F*ocus on delegating
instead of doing.

*G*oals are dreams
with deadlines.

*P*rovide the sky in which
others can soar.

*K*eep asking questions
and listen closely to
the answers.

*L*eaders see more in
other people than other people
see in themselves.

*P*raise in public.
Criticize in private.

*M*ilquetoast leadership
is not the breakfast
of champions.

*T*rue leaders put the
common good ahead
of personal gain.

*P*erform for results,
not recognition.

*F*ailure to take a risk is
much worse than taking a
risk that leads to failure.

*Y*our worst decision is the
one that is never made.

*P*utting ethics into practice
involves courage more
than conviction.

*G*ood leaders are both
born and made.

*I*f you grasp for power,
it will slip away.

$\mathcal{M}$ost solutions are simple.

$\mathcal{G}$ive employees some
breathing room.
Be "invisible" one day
every other week.

$\mathcal{L}$eaders understand
the power of synergy.

An in-person visit beats
a written memo every time.

A leader's state of mind
affects every person in
the organization.

A genuine show of
vulnerability often brings
great rewards.

*L*earn from the past,
focus on the present,
and prepare for the future.

*M*ake important decisions
only when you are
alert and relaxed.

*C*ontinually develop character
and competence.

*B*e teachable. You don't
know everything.

*R*ealize that knowledge
and skill are of no value without
the fuel of motivation.

*C*oercion kills the
corporate spirit.

The effective leader
instills commitment to,
not mere compliance with,
the shared vision.

A good leader is a person
of both action and intellect.

Listen to feedback carefully.

$\mathcal{A}$ willingness to
encourage change keeps
you moving forward.

$\mathcal{L}$ead people,
not organizations.

$\mathcal{R}$eserve fifteen minutes
a day for yourself for
uninterrupted quiet time.

A real leader wears
Velcro instead of Teflon where
acceptance of responsibility
is concerned.

*B*e willing to sacrifice.

"I care about you."
Say it, mean it, live it.

$\mathcal{M}$anage yourself;
lead others.

$\mathcal{T}$ake initiative and encourage
others to do the same.

$\mathcal{C}$ontinue to work on your
communication skills—
both written and verbal.

The path to success is
often illogical.

A timid employee is the
result of a tyrant.

Take charge without
always being in control.

*B*eware of shortcuts
when looking for ways
to minimize effort.

*B*e accessible and accountable.

*T*rust your gut feeling;
it's usually right.

A leader has a sense of humility.

A leader has a sense of history.

A leader has a sense of humor.

*T*rue sincerity is a rare
but valuable leadership trait.

*E*ach week select two items
from your to-do list and delegate
them to a capable employee.

*K*indness is not weakness.

$\mathcal{L}$ook at life through
the windshield, not the
rear-view mirror.

$\mathcal{E}$xpect people to
perform only as well as
the example you set.

$\mathcal{L}$ook for great ideas,
not just consensus.

$\mathcal{B}$e flexible.

$\mathcal{T}$rue leadership involves
not only the exercise of
authority but also full acceptance
of responsibility.

$\mathcal{V}$isit each associate's work
area at least once a month.

Uncertainties are a part of life.
Accept them.

A soft word turns away anger.

Ask your associates,
"What would you do?"
Expect powerful results.

*B*old leaders choose
the playing field over
the sidelines.

*S*et priorities and live by them.

*I*n solving a problem,
first look for flaws in
the organizational structure
rather than in the people.

*I*ntegrity and humility are
the leader's two best friends.

*G*ood leadership is much
deeper than personal
appearance or rhetoric.

*A*lways try to empower
others to do their best.

*S*hare your knowledge
with associates.

*E*ncourage decision-making
at all levels.

*G*ive others a second, third,
and fourth chance.

*F*ollow the channels
of authority. And remember
that it works both ways.

*S*mall acts of recognition
are very important.

*B*e firm but fair.

*A*void the quick fix.

*B*efore you critique another's behavior, list five positive things about that person.

*L*ook for ways to make other people's jobs more challenging and fulfilling.

*A*nticipate chaos and be prepared to work through it.

*D*ecisions should be based on the core values of an organization.

*L*eaders have an innate ability to bring out the best in others.

*R*ealize that a house
divided will fall.

*O*rganizations that encourage
everyone's participation have an
inside track to success.

*E*mployees want to be
heard and understood.

*P*rovide others with hope
for the future.

*D*evote your time and
energy to positive people and
positive thoughts.

*L*earn from failure. Don't
be crippled by it.

*Y*our rules apply to you, too.

*H*ave a genuine concern
for those you lead.

A leader living on the edge
might unwittingly push
others off the cliff.

Greet everyone with a smile and salutation each morning.

If you choose to chase mice, eventually you will get trampled by the elephants.

You are in partnership with the associates you serve.

*R*eal leaders are mentors.

*R*espect another's dignity.
Never blame or be judgmental.

A leader who is willing
to share the power enhances
consensus decision-making.

*L*isten with your heart as well
as your head.

*P*ut empathy ahead
of authority.

*U*se your drive time to
and from work to listen
to motivational tapes.

A good decision today
beats the "perfect" decision
next week.

*T*he path of least resistance
is not always the best choice.

A healthy organization
improves the lives of
its individuals.

*N*o decision should be
made in isolation.

*G*ive others the benefit
of the doubt.

*L*earn how to help others
achieve their full potential.

*P*lace effectiveness ahead
of efficiency.

*L*eadership is
about stewardship,
not ownership.

*B*e willing to laugh at yourself.

*S*end everyone home
two hours early one day
next week.

*C*hange three bad habits
a year—you will get
phenomenal results!

*B*e real. Others know
when you're just going through
the motions of good leadership.

The harder a leader pushes,
the more he or she pulls
the organization down.

Focus on guiding, not ruling.

Time and energy spent
worrying are wasted.

Seek wise counsel.

Giving associates a chance to
demonstrate their skills
will develop their confidence.

Willingly spend extra
time with those who
want to improve.

Continue to find new ways to support those around you.

Do not lower your standards to accommodate others.

Be willing to create openings for exceptional people, even when a position isn't currently available.

*E*xercise regularly.

*E*at properly.

*E*xamine your
health consistently.

Develop meaningful
relationships at every level.

Be courteous.

Emulate the leadership habits
of Vince Lombardi: discipline,
hard work, and commitment.

*I*f necessary, agree to disagree.

*N*ever use others for self-gain.

*A*void the temptation to blame outside circumstances for your problems.

A true leader trains
others to lead.

Keep a journal and write
in it daily.

An effective organization
functions as a community,
not as a family.

*T*rue loyalty is only that
which is volunteered.

*U*nderstand and support the
highest priorities of others.

*C*hallenges and tests go
with the territory.

Don't feel you have to do it all yourself.

Watch out for the "squeaky wheel."

Good leaders are not control freaks.

*E*nvision goals as the targets
and habits as the arrows.

*N*ever carry a grudge.

*T*he trick to getting angry
is not losing your temper.

*B*e willing to forgive
yourself, too.

*G*ive others credit for
your success.

*F*ailure sends a leader in
a new direction toward his
or her next success.

*O*ffer incentives that encourage
others to take risks.

*L*earn from the past
don't be paralyzed by it.

*R*ealize that we live
in the real world,
not an ideal one.

A reprimand should build up,
not tear down.

L ead a balanced life and
encourage the same in
those you lead.

B e willing to swim upstream.

Accept blame as well as fame.

Look for ways to relieve
stress in those around you.

Think of work as an adventure
and instill a sense of exploration
in others.

*U*nderstand the fragility
and importance of
others' self-esteem.

*I*nstill confidence, not
confusion, in those you lead.

*W*e are what we watch,
listen to, and read.

Remember to accept losing with dignity.

Remember that *silent* and *listen* contain the same letters.

An open-door policy should be exactly that.

Always focus on
the big picture.

Tackle problems by helping
associates choose solutions.

Put out a suggestion box,
read the contents once a week,
and act on them.

*U*se *we* instead of *me*.

*H*elp people produce
results they can be
proud of personally.

*A*lways keep in mind
that what others tell you is
only the tip of the iceberg.

Illustrate your spoken vision
with metaphors.

Be cognizant of the
unwritten rules that govern
the organization.

Be willing and prepared
to promote.

*Y*ou must earn respect,
not demand it.

*J*ust because you find
a problem doesn't mean
the system is broken.

*D*evelop a spirit of community,
one individual at a time.

If you feel your associates
frequently let you down,
explore those feelings
with your mentor.

Share your joy with others.

A company's shared vision
must be in harmony with
the personal visions of
its individuals.

*L*eaders are originals,
not duplicates.

*B*e there when needed,
not only when it is convenient.

A shared philosophy and
shared experiences sharpen
your team's cohesion.

*C*hoose what is right instead of
what is politically correct.

*C*onsult your conscience.

*T*he art of persuasion
begins with an open mind
and open ears, not
an open mouth.

*L*eaders often take
the unconventional road.

*K*now the difference
between a rash decision
and a prompt one.

*T*ell those you lead
what they need to hear,
not what you think they
want to hear.

$\mathcal{B}$e people-serving,
not self-serving.

$\mathcal{U}$se a variety of stories
and anecdotes to convey
the organization's history
and philosophy.

$\mathcal{R}$oll up your sleeves and
get your hands dirty.

*I*nside every person are
seeds of greatness.
Your task is to cultivate them.

*A*ccept responsibility
for those you lead.

*E*nthusiasm is a way of life,
not an emotion.

*A*n apology is the sign
of a secure leader.

*M*anagers rely on manuals.
Leaders rely on instinct.

*W*alk a mile in another
person's shoes before
passing judgment.

*A*ccept people for who
and what they are,
regardless of how different
they are from you.

*B*e aware of an associate's
obstacles to success and work
together to find the answers.

*S*tand tall through it all.

*N*ever put others on
the firing line until
they are ready.

*A*llow ample time for reflection
and dreaming.

*A*lways appear calm and cool,
never confused.

*B*e quick to throw a
lifeline to someone about
to be swept under.

A good leader aspires
to be a role model rather
than a hero.

*T*rust your judgment and
be willing to act on it.

*T*he abuse of power and
people will eventually
result in failure.

A good plan has a clearly
defined objective clearly
communicated to everyone.

*E*xert your will through
persuasion, not intimidation.

*P*ractice what you preach.

*M*istakes are a necessary part of the success process.

*P*otential results, when expressed, should fascinate and energize your team.

*L*earn to balance logic
and emotion.

*Y*ou must be yourself
to be at peace.

*E*very action should have
a clear purpose.

*F*ind your passion and
make it work toward
the common good.

*E*ncourage participation.

*P*ractice Stephen Covey's
three character traits of greatness:
integrity, maturity, and
abundance mentality.

*T*EAM means
"Together Everyone
Achieves More."

*E*mployees who are given
positive feedback work harder
and accomplish more.

*L*eaders look at others
as equals, not as subordinates.

*B*e consistently authentic
and genuine. If you lose
people's trust, it's almost
impossible to regain it.

A prudent leader understands
the risk/reward relationship.

*D*on't let your ego get
in the way.

The best concept cannot withstand poor leadership.

Respect those you serve.

True rapport within an organization cannot be developed without a commitment to truth.

*K*eep in touch with
the work being done.

*T*reat all that you do as
work in progress.

*S*hare both the work and
the wealth.

$\mathcal{L}$ook for the good in others.

$\mathcal{B}$uild camaraderie.

$\mathcal{A}$n organization's value
is measured as much by
the meaning it has for its
employees as it is by net profits.

$\mathcal{L}$earn the power of silence.

$\mathcal{E}$ncourage change and new ideas. Don't be intimidated by them.

$\mathcal{G}$ood leaders are like baseball umpires. They go practically unnoticed when doing their job right.

Small changes often
produce big results.

A group of people committed
to a shared vision can accomplish
the impossible.

The Book of
EXCELLENCE

*E*xcellence
is not optional.

*T*he new millennium will see
the death of the order taker.
Are you an order taker?

*P*roper planning
prevents poor performance.
Remember this as
the five *P*s.

*S*uccess at the expense
of faith and family
is really failure.

*B*e a team player.
Prima donnas don't last.

A good marketing plan
that does not generate
sales and profits is a failure.
Don't get the cart before
the horse.

True wisdom is not a fad.

Participate in a lead-sharing group. Suggested members: accountant, lawyer, developer, architect, telecommunications representative, marketing expert from your local chamber of commerce. This group will keep you in the know.

*D*evelop a sense of urgency to your work and pay attention to details.

*K*now your market. Where is the business? Who has it?

*D*o not put all your eggs (time) into one client's basket.

$\mathcal{M}$ake at least one new
account call per week.

$\mathcal{A}$lways ask for the order!
Don't worry about your
technique or style.

$\mathcal{P}$lan your sales
calls a minimum of one
week in advance.

*C*ustomers will always get what they want. The question is, "Will they get it from you?"

*A*rrogance is deadly.

*K*now where your sales increases will come from. They won't just happen!

*A*lways have five new target accounts in development.

*H*ave a single, consolidated planning calendar that you keep with you at all times.

*N*ever be too busy to follow up on the small things.

*M*anipulating outcomes never
provides the best results.

A bad attitude cancels all other
positive skills.

*D*on't go just for the big hit.
The greatest opportunities
exist in small- to
medium-sized companies.

Concentrate on your job,
not on everyone else's.

Be as critical of yourself
as you are of others.

Rely on your support staff.
Your time should be spent
in front of the customer,
not in the office.

*A*re you becoming
complacent?

*C*ustomers will find a way to buy
from you if they like you. They
will also find a way not to buy
from you if they don't like you.

*D*o you add value to your
customer's business?

$\mathscr{A}$lways carry an adequate supply of business cards.

$\mathscr{Y}$ou're not learning anything when you're talking.

$\mathscr{S}$et goals. Monitor your status on a quarterly basis. Modify your actions accordingly.

*E*ach day you get better
or worse. It's your choice.

*K*now your clients' hobbies.

*A*lways concentrate on
developing new business.
You never know when or
how you will lose one of
your key accounts.

*P*ush yourself.
Only you can motivate you.

*B*e a part of excellence,
not critical of it.

*D*on't be late for an
appointment. However,
it's all right for customers
to be late.

$\mathcal{B}$e open to change.

$\mathcal{C}$arry an adequate supply of change. You never know when you will need to feed the parking meter or use a pay telephone.

$\mathcal{B}$elieve in yourself, your company, your products.

*S*pend a minimum of four
hours per day in front
of customers.

*H*ave fun and celebrate
your successes.

*D*o your socks match your
suit? Don't wear light socks
with dark suits.

*G*od has given you another day.
Rejoice and be thankful!

*B*ecome actively involved
in your community through
a civic club.

*T*here is a wealth of
opportunity for the true
sales professional in
today's economy.

The best defense is still
a good offense.

Opportunities come in
unexpected packages.

Watch your jokes.
Make sure they are
wholesome and appropriate
for the audience.

*B*e yourself. You can't
fool the audience!

*G*reat potential is one of life's
heaviest burdens.

*B*e committed to your faith,
your family, and your
company—in that order.

*D*on't wear too much jewelry.

*D*on't get trapped at the purchasing agent level. Start at the top before progressing to the purchasing department.

*K*eep your competitors on their toes!

$\mathcal{B}$e nice.

$\mathcal{C}$ustomers love humility.

$\mathcal{A}$re there any sales training manuals, programs, books, or cassettes collecting dust on your shelves? Why? You can still learn from them.

Send your customers
plants or flowers on
special occasions.

Resist fads, whether in clothes
or language.

Send your clients copies
of news articles in which you
believe they have an interest.

*A*re your shoes polished?

*D*oes your belt match
your shoes?

*T*he top 20 percent
of sales producers earn
sixteen times more income
than the bottom 80 percent.

*G*et up early and work late.

*T*ell the truth!

*S*pend two hours at
home per week in creative
thinking, planning,
and working on
sales appointments.

$\mathscr{B}$e well manicured.

$\mathscr{B}$reakfast appointments
create sales opportunities.
Clients tend to be fresh
and more receptive then.

$\mathscr{F}$ollow the leader,
not the follower.

It is very important that
you like yourself.

Plan the following week
by this Friday.

Mediocrity is an
organizational disease.
Don't tolerate it!

$\mathcal{S}$et your watch ahead
five minutes. You will be
on time and will experience
less stress.

$\mathcal{D}$on't waste your
energy on gossip.

$\mathcal{E}$xpect excellence from yourself
and from others.

$\mathcal{B}$e serious about your business.

$\mathcal{W}$atch your weight.

$\mathcal{C}$heck the Help Wanted section. This will help you identify the most progressive companies. They are always excellent sales leads.

$\mathcal{G}$ive business leads to
professional associates.
Most likely, they will
return the favor.

$\mathcal{C}$all someone you haven't
seen for a while. Don't just
think about doing it.

$\mathcal{N}$ever take your business
relationships for granted.

Use all the resources available
to you. Solo performers
have a limited range.

Be loyal to your employer.

A customer's opinion is
formed within the first five
minutes after you meet.

*H*ave a professional,
but not necessarily expensive,
wardrobe.

*I*f you consistently have to
be the cheapest to get
the order, you are not a
professional salesperson.

*D*on't handle administrative
duties during prime selling time.

*R*eserve the middle of
the day and luncheons
for your clients.

*M*onday mornings
and Friday afternoons should be
work time, not wasted time.

*W*rite it down. Don't
rely on your memory.

*S*eek advice from
successful people.

*E*xpect others to make
appointments with you.
Your time is important.

*B*efore you sell it, make
sure you can service it!

*K*nowledge without
application is useless.

*B*e a student of your
industry: trends, competition,
niche opportunities.

*A*sk questions and
identify needs before
you present solutions.

*U*nderpromise and
overperform.

*I*f you follow up,
you will be a hero.

*D*o you add enough value to
more than compensate for the
difference you charge over your
competitor's lower price?

*B*eware of those who drop in.
They tend to waste time.

*L*isten. Listen. Listen.

*D*evelop relationships
with people at various
decision-making levels within
your accounts. Personnel
changes are inevitable.

*D*on't compete with
your customers.

*R*apport is not developed
on the telephone. Face-to-face
interaction develops long-term
business relationships.

*E*xcellence knows
no time clock.

Be present mentally, as well as physically, at meetings.

Good looks are truly only skin deep. Performance is lasting.

Ask your customers to audit your performance. Their opinion is the only one that truly matters.

𝒰nderstand the difference
between price and value.

𝒲atch those buzzwords!
They probably do not
mean the same to your
clients as they do to you.

𝒩ever compromise
on hiring quality!

$\mathcal{A}$sk your customers
for sales leads.

$\mathcal{A}$re you doing the same
things this year that you
did last year? If so,
you are losing ground.

$\mathcal{M}$otivation is what turns
knowledge and skill into success.

*I*f you were your own competitor, how would you win over your accounts?

*B*e a strong number two at your competitors' accounts.

*S*end birthday and anniversary cards.

Don't leave an opening for competition.

Technology is not a replacement for hard work.

Do your clothes or breath reek of smoke? Your customers will find this offensive.

*A*ll play and no work
does not work.

*W*hen you work hard,
you have earned the
right to play.

*D*oes your company
consider you profit or overhead?
Hope it's not the latter!

Don't slack up after a big sale. Turn it up another notch.

Emulate the habits of the winners, not the also-rans.

Make sure your customers know your product and service capabilities. It's amazing how many do not.

Strive to make yourself
and your company number one.

Solicit feedback from your
competitors' accounts. This
is very useful for identifying
ways to penetrate them.

Timing is everything.
Let it happen naturally.

*N*ever say negative things
about your company to
your clients. Instead,
communicate your concerns
to your management.

*W*ork harder and smarter.

*E*stablish an exercise routine.
This is important to your mental
well-being.

*Y*ou have a choice between
developing good habits
and bad habits.

*C*arry your business card file.
You never know when you will
need a telephone number.

*I*s your hair shaggy and unruly?
Is it too long? Do you use too
much hair spray?

Customers are looking for relationships, not transactions.

Dress conservatively. It still conveys an image of dependability and responsibility.

He who sows sparingly will also reap sparingly, and he who sows bountifully will also reap bountifully."
2 Corinthians 9:6

*S*end a plant to your customer's open house. It still works.

*C*arry an adequate supply of cash. Restaurants don't always take credit cards, and it is embarrassing to ask your customer to pay.

*A*re your clothes losing their crispness?

Watch the amount of
liquor you consume.
Your credibility could be
lost in one evening.

Tell your vendors who
behave professionally how
much you appreciate them.

Take an active, not passive,
role in helping your community.

*O*bserve five habits of a successful salesperson you know.

*D*on't spend your time worrying about why you can't win an account. Concentrate your thoughts on how you can win it.

*I*f you are a veteran, learn from the rookies.

Make two morning and two afternoon appointments your minimum daily goal.

Silence is a necessity, not a negative.

What percentage of your customers' total business are you receiving?

*D*on't confuse efforts
with results.

*A*re you presenting new
ideas or concepts to your
clients? If not, your competition
will and you will lose.

*P*assion is the pulse
of customer service.

Avoid "canned" presentations.
They are boring.

Don't talk down to
your customers.

Use a beeper. That will
let the office get in touch
with you when a customer
needs you in an emergency.

*M*easure three times,
cut once.

*S*ell your customers what
they want, not what you
think they need.

*D*o you thoroughly know
the features and benefits
of your products?

*D*on't give away the farm!

*C*heck your breath before
you meet your customers.

*R*eserve a weekly luncheon
or breakfast for your spouse
and children. This time will be
more important to them than
your business successes.

*D*on't wear cheap cologne or perfume. And don't use an overpowering amount.

*P*roofread all correspondence!

*D*o you feel the customer is fortunate to do business with you? You better not!

*R*emember, it is harder to
keep an account than
it was to get it.

*B*e nice to secretaries.

*D*o what you said you were
going to do, when you said you
were going to do it, and how you
said you were going to do it.

*L*et your support staff
know how special and
important they are. Be sincere
when you tell them!

*C*ustomers buy enthusiasm!

*M*ake appointments.
Remember, your client's
time is very important.

$\mathscr{M}$uch potential business
and better profit opportunities
exist in rural areas because
most of your competitors
stay in cities.

$\mathscr{T}$ake time to sharpen your saw.

$\mathscr{D}$on't expect prime accounts
to be handed to you. Be
proactive and develop
new business.

𝒫articipate in a fellowship group.

𝒟on't expect your customers
to tell you they are unhappy
with your level of service.

𝒮pend as much time
providing customer service
as you do talking about it.

*D*o you create sales
opportunities or just
react to them?

*S*trive for increases in profits,
not just sales volume.

*I*t's not the big things you
do for your clients that make you
successful. It's the little things.

*B*e consistently persistent,
but not a pest.

*S*ales is not for everyone.
Don't feel you are a failure
if you try this profession
and it doesn't fit you.

*K*now how your products
differ from those of
your competitors.

*I*nvest your time in learning,
not just in training.

*S*top, listen, and think
before you respond.

*D*evelop and commit to
memory ten questions that
will help you identify
a customer's needs.

*I*f you're not changing,
you're not in first place.

*S*mile. Customers like
positive people.

*W*hen you are out of the office,
call for messages at 10:00 A.M.,
2:00 P.M., and 4:00 P.M.

Aim high. You normally
hit what you aim for.

Relationships require more
than one sales call.

Don't dump all your
products on your clients.
Identify their primary needs
and submit your solutions.

*D*on't tell your customer how good you are. Show them!

*Y*our chances for success increase in proportion to the number of sales calls you make.

*B*e concerned when you lose, but don't let it defeat you.

*T*arget accounts that fit
your profile for the
optimum customer.

*H*ave an objective for
each sales call.

*R*ead *Living Above
the Level of Mediocrity*
by Chuck Swindoll.
(Word, 1987)

$\mathcal{M}$ake that extra
call at 4:30 P.M.

$\mathcal{S}$top in the bathroom before
your presentation. This is an
excellent time to check your
breath and appearance.

$\mathcal{A}$ nice car is not the key to
success. The key is the driver.

*I*nvest your time in
customers who have
the financial ability to purchase
your products or services.

*Y*our time budget is
as important as your
financial budget.

*T*ake time to recharge your
batteries. Rest is important.

*N*ever accept mediocrity.

*B*e consistently aware of
how you are utilizing your time.
Conduct monthly audits.

*W*hat's your best remedy
when you are feeling down? Try
making several new sales calls.
You will be amazed at the results.

Congratulate your peers
on their accomplishments.

Mend broken relationships.
Negative energy will keep
you from being productive.

If you want to impress your
customers, make written notes
when they respond to
your questions.

Improve your speaking skills
by enrolling in Toastmasters
or by attending a
Dale Carnegie course.

Thank your spouse for
his or her help and support.

Patience is a virtue.
Don't give up.

Sales is like banking. You have to make the deposits before you can participate in the withdrawals.

Don't be an underachiever.

Schedule daily quiet time for planning, relaxing, and brainstorming.

*A*lways keep social and
business relationships separate.

*C*oncentrate on sales,
not on marketing.

*B*elieve in yourself.
If you don't, who will?

Be aggressive,
but not oppressive!

If you smoke, don't light
up in front of your customers.

Keep your car, especially
the interior, clean at all times.

$\mathcal{M}$ove fast.

$\mathcal{R}$emember that none of us is more important than the team.

$\mathcal{D}$on't keep doing the wrong things over and over. Learn from your mistakes and take another approach.

$\mathcal{D}$on't be too comfortable.

$\mathcal{I}$nvite your customers out
for a glass of iced tea or
lemonade. You will be amazed
at how much they enjoy
the simple pleasures.

$\mathcal{D}$on't waste your time on
conceptual training. Be practical.

*A*sk for help.

*I*f you can't find the time
to do it right the first time,
how will you find the time
to do it over and over?

*T*here is no replacement
for effort.

*H*old annual feedback
sessions with your customers.
You will be amazed
at the benefits.

*S*uccess does not come
easily. Are you willing to
pay the price?

*E*xcellence usually
takes a little longer.

Satisfaction
GUARANTEED

The three keys to customer service excellence are quality people, quality products, quality systems.

Listen twice as much as you talk.

Once you lose customers to bad customer service, it is almost impossible to get them back.

*N*ever argue with a customer who wants a refund or an exchange.

*C*ustomer service is either good or bad. There is no in-between.

*I*f you provide only 99 percent satisfaction, a million transactions mean ten thousand unhappy customers.

*O*ffer your customers at least one service they cannot get anywhere else.

*H*ow many customers did you lose last year due to poor customer service?

*A*nswer the phone by the third ring.

Don't be afraid to lose money to satisfy a customer. Short-term losses can equal long-term gains.

Response time should be measured in minutes, not hours.

If management doesn't care about customer service, employees won't either.

*D*on't accept mediocrity!

*I*f your departments don't communicate effectively with each other, you can be sure they aren't communicating with your customers either.

*C*ustomers want to feel important.

*H*ire nice people.

*B*y providing excellent customer service, you can increase sales to your existing accounts by 30 percent.

*M*ake sure your voice mail is not voice jail.

The receptionist is the "Director of First Impressions"! Hire and train appropriately.

Never keep customers on hold for more than thirty seconds.

A negative attitude cancels out all positive skills.

*I*t's easier to get customers
than it is to keep them.

*T*oll-free customer service
lines should not be a substitute
for personal contact.

*D*evelop ways to measure
your level of customer service.

If possible, return all phone calls within one hour.

Remember, little things make a big difference.

This year improve your performance in at least three areas to serve your customers better.

*S*tudy companies with
impressive service reputations,
such as L. L. Bean or
Federal Express.

*E*mpower all employees
to serve your customers.

*C*ustomer service is high touch,
not high tech.

*N*ever tell a customer,
"That's not my job!"

*C*ustomers communicate
with their wallets.

*T*ell your customers how
much you appreciate them,
then show them.

*N*ever be too busy to follow up on your customers' requests.

*N*ever argue with a customer.

*T*he difference between outstanding and mediocre service is the discretionary effort of loyal employees.

The best vehicle to develop increased sales is a first-rate customer service program.

Follow up, follow up, follow up.

Most customers don't take the time to complain. They just leave and never return!

*A*lways tell the truth.

*G*ive the customer service
department complete
responsibility and authority
to make immediate decisions.

*N*o employee is exempt
from serving your customers.

Read at least one biography
of a successful business
leader this year.

High employee turnover
always results in poor
customer service.

Customers should "hear" your
smile over the phone.

*C*onsult customers before introducing new products or services.

*E*xcellent customer service equals long-term success.

*A*sk your customers how you're doing. Theirs are the only answers that matter.

Terminate employees with
bad attitudes.

Be as interested in the
appetizers as you are in the
entrées. (Customers won't give
large orders if you can't
handle small ones.)

Indifference is deadly.

*T*ake action immediately when you hear of a customer service problem.

*N*ever forget the basics.

A customer should never have to talk to more than two people for assistance: the receptionist and a customer service representative.

*N*ever, ever forget the customer.

*S*hare customer service
feedback with your employees
on a regular basis.

*Y*our corporate culture should
be built around customer
service excellence, not
products or service.

*C*ustomer service is much
more than a slogan.

*T*he service excellence formula:
Excellent Employees equals
Excellent Service.

*E*ncourage those who
communicate with customers by
phone to meet them personally.

*P*eople buy from people,
not from machines.

*D*on't waste your time
trying to change employees
who have bad attitudes. Hire
people with good attitudes.

*U*se the mystery shopper
audit system.

*B*e honest. Would you buy from your company?

*C*ustomers will pay more for excellent service.

*I*f you want your business to grow, do the best job of serving customers in your industry.

*H*old meetings in which
your customers explain what
they expect from their suppliers.

*L*ower prices do not justify
poor customer service.

A positive image is
very important.

"May I help you?"
(with a smile) is still in vogue.

Old-fashioned customer
service still works.

Customers should expect
consistent quality and never
have to settle for mediocrity.

If you promise the moon,
be able to deliver it.

*S*mall companies have an
advantage in maintaining
a philosophy of customer
service excellence.

*Y*our first chance may
be your last.

*E*ven one employee who fails
to buy into your customer service
program will hurt the results.

*N*ever say, "I don't know."
It is your responsibility to know.

*C*ustomers should never
be made to feel they are
bothering you by expecting
excellent service.

*I*f customers don't receive
100 percent satisfaction, they
should not have to pay full price.

*R*eward your employees
for excellent customer service.

*A*t the end of the day,
ask yourself, "Are all of
my customers happy?"

*M*ake sure all departments
work together in pleasing
your customers.

*C*ustomer service programs
aren't expensive to implement.

A customer should never
have to search for help.

"Satisfaction guaranteed or your money back" was once the benchmark of one of the best service companies in America.

Customer service should be fun.

The customer's perception of the situation is reality.

*W*hen employees love
their jobs, customers feel
the winning spirit.

*A*ccept the challenge of
satisfying the most
difficult customers.

*P*oor customer service
is the root of the problems
of most companies.

*D*on't become so focused
on new ideas and new
customers that you forget
the ideas and people who
got you where you are.

*T*he receptionist should
not put customers on hold.

*L*et common sense prevail.

*P*rior to making decisions,
put yourself in your
customers' shoes.

*N*ever be satisfied.

*W*hen you provide good
service, your customers are
the first to benefit.

*W*ithout attention to
excellent customer service,
even a good marketing
plan will fail.

*T*he best technology in the
world will never overcome the
bad attitude of one employee.

*C*ustomer service never
goes out of style.

The three *Cs* of customer service excellence are Care, Concern, Compassion.

Excellent service organizations always keep their promises.

No Trust equals
No Confidence equals
No Business.

*Y*ou need your customers
more than they need you.

*M*anagement needs to spend
time listening to customers.

*A*s successful companies
grow, practices change
but principles remain.

*S*uccessful service organizations
are always reinventing
and are never satisfied.

*C*ustomers hate to hear,
"I'm sorry, but they're
in a meeting."

*K*eep customer service
surveys brief and pay careful
attention to them.

The heart of customer
service excellence is people,
not economics.

Have someone available to
handle customer service
calls during all hours of
the business day.

One act of indifference can
destroy a relationship forever.

*W*hen you start taking
your customers for granted,
you start losing them.

*D*on't just talk about it. Do it!

*D*o your customers feel
that you truly appreciate
their business? Ask them.

*B*reak bread with
your customers.

*T*he customer service
budget is as important as
the advertising budget.

*D*on't focus on developing
new business until you can
effectively service your
existing customers.

$\mathcal{G}$ood isn't good enough!

$\mathcal{S}$et high customer service goals. Monitor and modify them constantly.

$\mathcal{N}$ever think you and your company are more important than your customers.

*R*emember, customers
have choices.

*T*he customer's confidence
is a powerful asset.

*C*ustomer service requires
a twenty-four-hour-a-day,
seven-days-a-week commitment.

The receptionist is one of
the most important
customer service persons
in your organization.

Remember, happy employees
result in satisfied customers.

Quite simply, the integrity
of an organization is the
soul of service.

*N*ever underestimate the intelligence of a customer.

*S*pend as much time on customer service training as you do on sales training.

*G*enuinely care about your customers.

If you don't like people,
you shouldn't be in business.

*S*ales gets customers;
service keeps them.

*H*ave a toll-free customer
service line, preferably open
twenty-four hours a day.

ake all your
customers feel as if they're
the most important.

*D*on't bother customers
during their busy times.

ake sure customer opinion
surveys have prepaid postage.
Customers should not have to
pay to give you their opinions.

*D*o your competitors offer
superior customer service?
Match them or get ready
to be second best.

*W*hen you make a mistake,
correct it immediately.

*C*ustomer service is
everyone's job.

*N*ever have customers
wait for employees who
are on personal calls.

*D*on't get so hung up on
administrivia that you ignore
the customer.

*K*now what happens
once your company receives
a complaint.

*C*onsistently share articles
and books on customer service
with your staff.

*D*on't be too proud to say,
"I'm sorry!"

*T*alking about customer
service is not the same
as providing it.

Handle complaints promptly.

Stay in touch with your customers to be certain they are happy with your products and services.

Ask customers what they want. Then deliver it.

*D*elegate decision-making
ability; minimize the
need for approvals.

*E*xceed your customers'
expectations.

*T*estimonials about excellent
service are the most effective
advertisements.

Communicate, communicate, communicate.

Customers want solutions, not excuses.

What happens to the information your customer service reps collect?

*H*appy customers tell few;
unhappy customers tell many.

*Y*ou will never be the best
if your customer service
is less than exceptional.

*D*o the simple things in an
exceptional way.

*D*on't let prosperity cloud your objectivity about how customers see you.

*S*atisfied customers equal profits.

*M*inimize the paperwork required to solve your customers' problems.

*C*ustomer satisfaction is an art.

*W*ell-treated employees treat customers well.

*I*f you want honest answers from your employees and customers, keep their responses in strict confidence.

Out hustle your competition.

No matter how large your
company, treat customers
as if your survival depends
on them. It does.

Get to know your customers
on a first-name basis.

*N*ever justify a problem.
Fix it instead.

*I*f your company isn't growing, it
could be the result of poor-to-
mediocre customer service.

*B*e calm when dealing
with problems.

*I*f you have high customer turnover, you're doing a poor job of serving your customers.

*E*stablish a minimum response goal, and then live by it.

*T*here is a wealth of opportunity for those who please customers.

*W*arranties and guarantees should be unconditional.

*D*on't judge a book by its cover. Small customers become big customers.

*V*iew customers as people, not statistics.

*E*mployees will follow your
lead, good or bad.

*W*henever possible, do
business with your customers.

*F*or a business to be successful,
management must communicate
the company's mission to
all employees.

*M*ake sure you can service
what you sell prior to taking it
to the marketplace.

*P*oor service can make a
good product fail.

*C*ontinually seek ways to
improve your customer service.

*B*ureaucracy and customer service are mutually exclusive.

*C*ustomer service should be the top priority in your company, from the bottom to the top.

*S*ome of the greatest customer service ideas come from the least likely sources.

*R*eward employees who
excel at customer service.

*C*ustomers should have direct
access to top management.

*I*f you are first in customer
service, you can ultimately
be first in sales.

A warranty is only as good as you make it.

If you give bad service, customers will leave you without uttering a word.

Service is the highest value your customers are looking for.

*C*ustomers hate to hear,
"Can it wait until Monday?"

*C*ustomers love to hear,
"What can I do to help you?"

*I*f you substituted a
customer appreciation banquet
for the annual sales meeting, the
results would be staggering.

$\mathcal{B}$e creative and unconventional when solving your customers' problems.

$\mathcal{C}$ompensate your staff as much for keeping customers as you do for getting them.

$\mathcal{T}$oll-free customer service lines should be adequately staffed.

*Y*our customer service
standards should be well defined.

*B*e thankful for customers
who complain. You still have
the opportunity to make
them happy.

*M*any customers will
never call you back after
a bad experience.

*I*f you don't take care of your customers, your competitors will.

*I*f you're having a bad day, don't let your customers "feel" it!

*I*nclude your customers in your planning. You will be surprised at how much you learn.

*C*ustomers hate to wait.

*C*ustomers despise
incompetence.

*O*ccasionally have an employee
or family member order from
your competitors so you can
know how well they serve
their customers.

If you advertise it,
you better have it.

Develop a customer service
mission statement.
Communicate it and live it!

Reward customers for
referring new clients to you.

*D*on't expand too quickly.

*D*evelop ways to make your customers more profitable.

*A*sk your employees for input on how to better serve your customers. Their feedback will surprise you.

*Y*ou can never train your
staff too much.

*N*ever put your employees
on the firing line without
proper training.

*N*ever compromise quality
for a lower price.

*B*e sure that employees know and understand company policies and service contracts.

*H*ire a good mix of maturity and youth.

*M*anagement must practice what it preaches.

*R*emember, customers talk.

*Y*ou can learn how to improve
customer service when you
work out problems with
your own vendors.

*F*ill all orders before
the promised deadline.

*E*ducate customers on the
best ways to use your products
and services.

*S*ervice your own products;
free of charge is best.

*I*f you make an error, try
to correct it and notify your
customer before he or
she notices it.

*L*earn from your mistakes.

*W*hen you are offering a special price on an item, refund the difference to anyone who inadvertently paid full price.

*A*lways remember that no one knows your client's business better than he or she does.

*D*evelop a comprehensive
customer service
training program.

*A*ll employees should either
serve your customers or
assist those who do.

*P*ay attention to the future.
Anticipate the changing needs
of your customers.

*E*valuate what you're doing right, as well as what you're doing wrong.

*M*ake sure your support staff feels as important as your sales staff.

*C*orrect weaknesses before they become serious problems.

The only way to beat your competition consistently is to outservice them.

Say "Thank you" a lot.

The only goal for customer service is 100 percent customer satisfaction.

*F*ocus on treating people
with dignity and respect and
the bottom line will shine!

*T*he customer is always right.